TRAINER'S
Pocketfile
of Ready-To-Use **Activities**

A pocketful of powerful and
persuasive activities for
teambuilding and people skills
development, plus icebreakers,
energizers, spot-checks, quizzes
and universal exercise designs for
all types of learning event

John Townsend

Published by:

**Management
Pocketbooks Ltd**
Laurel House
Station Approach
Alresford
Hants
SO24 9JH
U.K.

Tel: +44 (0)1962 735573
Fax: +44 (0)1962 733637
E-mail: sales@pocketbook.co.uk
Website: www.pocketbook.co.uk

First published in 1993 as the Trainer's Pocketbook of Ready-To-Use Exercises. Second edition published in 1997, as the Trainer's Blue Pocketfile of Ready-To-Use Exercises. This edition published in 2005.

ISBN 1 903776 37 6

British Library Cataloguing-in-Publication Data – a catalogue record for this book is available from the British Library.

Design, typesetting and graphics by **efex ltd**. Printed in the UK

CONTENTS

ICEBREAKERS & ENERGIZERS   5
- Meet my neighbour
- One sentence jobs
- The name game
- Two true one false
- Fantasy business cards
- Geography
- Prizes
- Congratulations!
- Famous partners
- 5 things I'm not!
- The story hat
- Bumper stickers
- This is me
- Vacations
- Jovial John
- Chinese portrait
- First records
- Getting here
- Stick-up needs
- Who's the trainer?

UNIVERSAL EXERCISE DESIGNS   29
- ClusterCards
- Mind mapping
- Vernissage
- T-shirt recap
- Newspaper headlines

SPOT-CHECKS   35
- Happy?
- Speed of course?
- Interest/usefulness
- Theory/practice
- Content/instructor/facilities
- Results/effort/satisfaction

TEAMBUILDING ACTIVITIES   43
- Jobscaping
- Building a skills inventory
- Leadership expectations
- Building trust & confidence
- Problem-solving (Who does what?)
- Creative thinking (Archaeology, Ties, Atlantis)

WESTREK   57
Transport your participants to the Wild West in this survival activity that teaches the essentials of project planning.

FOREST FIRE   83
An activity to practise consensus-seeking and study the impact of attitudes and values on team decision-making.

TESTS & QUIZZES   99
- Questionnaires
- Recap test
- Recap quiz game
- Superstar test & action plan
- The 7 wonders memory test

HOW TO USE THE CD

To undertake the activities in this Pocketfile you will, in most cases, need to prepare participant handouts. Instructions on doing so can be found in this book, at the beginning of each of the applicable activities.

To help you prepare professional-looking handouts we have bundled with this Pocketfile a CD ROM which contains the Team Instruction Cards, Maps, Clue Cards and other materials required for the activities. Look out for this logo:

Simply insert the CD into your disc drive and, on a **PC**, it should automatically start. If this is not the case, access the CD via Windows Explorer or File Manager. On **Apple Macs** access the CD via your desktop and double click on the Blue-pocketfile icon.

With the CD loaded, click on the relevant chapter or activity to find the images you wish to print off.

We recommend that you print from your laser or inkjet printer on to fairly thick paper of about 160 gsm. Such paper is available in a range of colours, so you can give each of your participating teams a set of handouts in a different colour.

Often there will be two or more images to an A4 page so have some scissors or a retractable knife handy in order to trim the cards to size (follow the trim guidelines printed on the page).

If your PC crashes and you're in a hurry, don't panic because you can photocopy the handouts from the pages of this book!

1CEBREAKERS
& ENERGIZERS

ICEBREAKERS & ENERGIZERS

ABOUT THIS SECTION

The following activities can be used as:

- **Icebreakers** at the beginning of a course to get things off to a good start, accelerate trainee participation and make sure everyone feels included (sometimes called *inclusion activities*) or as...

- **Energizers** at any time during a training course when you feel that the energy level in the room is dropping, people are losing concentration or that the group's cohesion is not what it should be

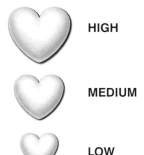

HIGH

MEDIUM

LOW

I have classified each activity as being high, medium or low *effect*. In other words, how much *heart* (self-revelation) does the exercise ask of participants? How embarrassing might it be for someone to participate? You should choose an icebreaker/energizer which has a heart level that fits with the amount of self-revelation which will be required of participants during the rest of the course.

MEET MY NEIGHBOUR

1. Make sure that each participant has a pen and a notepad and ask each of them to interview their neighbour (five minutes each way) concentrating their questions in two to three specific areas. For instance:

LOW

   - Job title and responsibilities
   - Family and hobbies
   - Course-related experience, training needs

2. Ask each participant (in turn or at random) to present their neighbour. ('This is Jack Fry and he's a systems analyst from C division')

   - If there is an odd number of participants the trainer should interview the *odd man out* and vice versa.

ICEBREAKERS & ENERGIZERS
ONE SENTENCE JOBS

LOW

1. Make sure that each participant has a pen and notepad and ask each of them to describe their job to their neighbour. The objective is for the neighbour to write down a satisfactory description of the job **in one sentence only**.

2. Ask each participant (in turn or at random) to read out the one sentence description of their neighbour's job. Ask for comments or questions from the job-holder and/or other participants.

   ● If there is an odd number of participants the trainer should interview the *odd man out* and vice versa.

Developed by Mervyn Simmonds

ICEBREAKERS & ENERGIZERS
THE NAME GAME

This icebreaker works best when tables are in a U-shape.

MEDIUM

1. Ask participants to hide their name plates.

2. Explain that they are going to participate in a fast-moving and effective exercise to help remember everyone's name. Starting with the first person on the trainer's left, each person must call out the names of all the people to his/her right in turn and then clearly say his/her name. Demonstrate by saying, 'This is Susan and I'm John'. Point out that the task gets progressively more difficult as it goes on. Susan obviously has the mammoth task of remembering everyone's name!

3. Each time a participant can't remember a name, ask the forgotten one to say it again loud and clear.

    ● No winners or losers!

TWO TRUE ONE FALSE

1. Ask each participant to write down three things about themselves. Two should be true and one false. For example: *I'm a keen cyclist, I was born in Scotland and I love Camembert* (for someone born in Wales).

2. Choosing at random, ask participants to state the three things and then invite the others to say which one they think is untrue.

   ● Use every opportunity to get participants to enlarge on true or false statements and encourage humour in order to accelerate the icebreaking process

MEDIUM

10

FANTASY BUSINESS CARDS

1. Ask each participant to take a few moments to fantasise about the name they wish they'd been born with and the job or profession they've always dreamed of having, and to create their fantasy business card. For example, someone might want to be:

HIGH

Or

CLINT FOX
MOUNTAINEER

25 Peak Road,
Snowdonia National Park, North Wales

Tania Chekov
BALLET DANCER

11 Stage Avenue,
Kensington Road, London W8

2. Ask for volunteers, or choose participants at random, to read out and explain some of the reasons for their business cards.

●   Use every opportunity for light-hearted banter with extrovert participants

●   Boost introverts with favourable comments on choice

GEOGRAPHY

LOW

1. Depending on the diversity of participants' backgrounds, draw a rough map of the world, country or region on the whiteboard or flip chart before the course starts.

2. As soon as everyone is present, ask each participant (in turn or at random) to come up, mark their home town on the map and give a one-minute description of the town and/or their childhood.

    ●   Ask people from the same place to *compare notes*

    ●   Encourage other participants to ask questions

ICEBREAKERS & ENERGIZERS

PRIZES

1. Ask each participant to describe to the group:
   - **One thing I have 'won'** (trophies, prizes, esteem, friendship, personal combats, etc)
2. Ask questions and encourage other participants to do so.
   - Encourage shy participants with friendly reinforcement
   - Exchange banter with extroverts

HIGH

CONGRATULATIONS!

HIGH

1. Ask participants to write down their most significant accomplishment over the last six months (private or professional) and explain it to their neighbour.

2. Ask participants (in turn or at random) to boast about the accomplishment of their neighbour in order to merit the **10 seconds of compulsory applause** which the other participants must give after the brief description of each exploit.

ICEBREAKERS & ENERGIZERS

FAMOUS PARTNERS

LOW

1. Prepare Post-it notes per participant, each with the name of one of a famous couple (eg: Adam & Eve, Bonny & Clyde, Romeo & Juliet).

2. Before you start the course, quickly circle round the class and stick a name on each participant's back.

3. State: 'Before we start the course, you must find your *partner!*'

Rules: since they cannot see who they are, they must ask questions of other participants who may only answer with *yes* or *no* (eg: 'Am I a film star?'...., 'Yes'...., 'Stan Laurel?'...., 'No').

4. As soon as partners have found each other they sit down at their original places.

   - If there is an odd number of participants make one set of cards a trio (eg: Marx Brothers, Three Musketeers, etc).

ICEBREAKERS & ENERGIZERS

5 THINGS I'M NOT!

MEDIUM

1. Ask participants (in turn or at random) to tell the class five things which they are not. I have rated this exercise medium *heart* since participants are free to choose how self-revealing they want to be.

● Example of a relatively low *heart* contribution: 'I'm not Turkish. I'm not a football fan. I'm not rich. I'm not married. I'm not on vacation nor am I a fish lover'.

● Example of shared strong feelings (high *heart*): 'I'm not feeling happy. I'm not sure why the hell I've been sent on this course. I'm not looking forward to it. I'm not in favour of video role-plays and I am not a supporter of this kind of exercise'.

THE STORY HAT

LOW

1. Ask each participant in turn (five minutes each way) to interview their neighbour to discover a success or failure story concerning the course subject matter.
    Examples:
    - The worst customer service I've experienced in the last year
    - The best manager I ever met

2. Ask participants, with their neighbour's help, to find a title for their story and write it on a slip of paper (anonymous). Examples:
    - The Disastrous Car Hire
    - Mr Wonderful

3. Collect the slips of paper in a hat.

4. Ask someone to pick one *blind*, read out the title and ask if the anonymous author would be willing to tell the story. If no answer, pick another (therefore low *heart*).

5. Continue for as long as time allows.

ICEBREAKERS & ENERGIZERS

BUMPER STICKERS

MEDIUM

Most participants will have seen the kind of bumper sticker which proclaims what the driver of the car would rather be doing: *'I'd rather be sailing'*, etc.

1. Ask each participant to create their own mental bumper sticker by telling the others what they'd rather be doing than sitting in the classroom today.

2. The rule is that no one can say that there's nothing they'd rather be doing than attending your course!

3. Encourage people to expand on their hobbies or other alternative activities. Play along with participants who pretend to be *anti* and explore reasons with real gripers.

ICEBREAKERS & ENERGIZERS
THIS IS ME

HIGH

1. From the accompanying CD, print off one 'empty' picture frame per participant.

2. Give each participant a picture frame and at least one coloured marker.

3. Ask each participant to create a self-portrait in any way they see fit (drawing, logo, phrase, abstract design, etc).

4. Collect the papers and display them on a board.

5. Ask each participant (in turn, at random or by volunteering) to identify their portrait and say a few words about why they have represented themselves in that way.

● Allow shy participants to *pass* at any stage. However, the exercise is high *heart* since to *pass* is, in itself, self-revealing!

VACATIONS

MEDIUM

1. Ask participants to think back to the best vacation they have ever had.

2. Ask each person (in turn, at random or by volunteering) to describe their vacation **in not more than 30 seconds**.

3. Note each vacation with a key word and a number on the flip chart (eg: 1. Spain, 2. Alps, etc), leaving a *scoring* column on the right.

4. After the last description, ask each person to vote for the vacation which they would most like to have had (apart from their own!) and mark each person's vote in the score column.

5. Give a small prize to the winner. Something fun such as an imitation Travel Agency certificate will help create a relaxed atmosphere.

JOVIAL JOHN

MEDIUM

1. Ask participants to think of an adjective which begins with the same letter as the initial of their first name and which describes either their personality or the way they are feeling right now! Examples:

   - Jovial John, Melancholy Mary, Serious Sam, Happy Harry, Worried Wendy, etc.

2. Invite them (in turn or by volunteering) to tell the others which name they've chosen and why.

- This one is only medium *heart* because people can choose to be as bold or as bland as they like with their alliteration. But they must say something!

CHINESE PORTRAIT

The French call this one a *Chinese Portrait*.

1. Ask participants to think about what they would be if they were…(choose one or two):
   - An animal, a tree, a car, a song, etc

2. Ask them (in turn or by volunteering) to explain to the class what they have chosen and why.

VARIATION

1. Ask participants to describe their neighbour or any other member of the group as an animal, a car, etc, and to give their reasons.

- This version is extra high *heart* and should only be used in courses where interactive behaviour and interpersonal communication are on the programme.

HIGH

23

ICEBREAKERS & ENERGIZERS
FIRST RECORDS

Just about everyone likes some kind of music and musical tastes can speak louder than words!

1. Ask participants to introduce themselves by telling the others about the first record they ever bought and why!

2. Encourage them to talk either about the evolution of their musical tastes since then or to highlight what they were doing at the time of their first record. They could even trace their careers (briefly!) by referring to subsequent records.

MEDIUM

ICEBREAKERS & ENERGIZERS
GETTING HERE

LOW

1. Ask participants to introduce themselves by explaining how they got to the training room (mode of transport, route taken, etc).

● This provides an opportunity for friendly banter with extroverts as well as the chance to boost the confidence of the shyer participants.

STICK-UP NEEDS

LOW

1. Make sure that all participants have a broad marker and a card (minimum size A5) or Post-it note.

2. Play some relaxing music and ask them all to write down '**three things I want to have happened to me by the end of this course**'. Encourage people to write down things like: 'to have learned how to ...., to have improved my ...., to have understood ....', etc, and to put their name on the card.

3. Collect the cards and stick them on a board or flip chart (if not self-adhesive, use masking tape or spray glue).

4. Ask people at random to expand on their needs and make extra notes for yourself as necessary.

ICEBREAKERS & ENERGIZERS

WHO'S THE TRAINER?

LOW

An extra-low heart one to end with!

1. Simply ask participants, either after some written preparation or directly, to try and guess things about **YOU the trainer!**

2. Depending on how much they know about you already, you may want to ask them to guess:
   - What car you drive
   - Your astrological sign
   - Where you went on your last vacation
   - What you did at the weekend
   - Where you live, etc

This icebreaker *protects* the shy participant who doesn't have to shout out his/her guesses but can still enjoy the fun where the trainer and not the participant is the butt of the humour.

NOTES

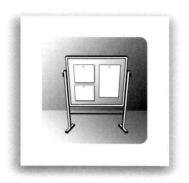

UNIVERSAL
EXERCISE DESIGNS

UNIVERSAL EXERCISE DESIGNS
CLUSTERCARDS

ClusterCards is quite simply a card-based learning puzzle for pairs or trios and is a useful method to discover the learning of steps, types or sequences especially with technical and/or potentially boring subjects.
Great also for Gap Analysis or…. RECAPS!

1. Choose something you teach which has a number of related steps, phases or types. These could be sequential or stand alone.

   EXAMPLES
   - 4 levels of training evaluation
   - 4 steps in a sales call
   - 3 new products and their related features/benefits
   - 10 steps to training transfer

2. For each step, phase or type, create a set of ClusterCards. Each set should contain a (differently designed) title card and three or four descriptive cards. Taking the FORM, STORM, NORM and PERFORM phases of team development as an example, you could create a set of 16 ClusterCards – a title card for each of the 4 phases and a further 3 descriptive cards for each phase. Or, you might choose to highlight the different features of 3 new products. In this instance you would prepare 4 ClusterCards per product – a title card plus 3 descriptive cards – giving a total of 12 ClusterCards.

3. Ask pairs or trios to complete the clusters by placing the cards in the right order on a table-top or pre-prepared board and award a prize for finishing first. Get them to self-correct by giving out an 'answer sheet'.

MIND MAPPING

Asking participants to create a mind map is a great way to find out what they know (before a session) or to recap what they remember (after a session) about any topic.

These days, most people know the basic principles of mind mapping (ie: start with the name of the topic in the centre and build keywords and images onto *branches* and then *twigs* stemming from the branches).

- Break the group into teams of 3-5 and assign a pinboard/whiteboard/*landscape* flip chart sheet
- Ask each team to produce a creative and detailed keyword/image representation of the topic

 Instead of asking them to present their mind map to the other teams, why not do a *Vernissage*? (see next page)

UNIVERSAL EXERCISE DESIGNS

VERNISSAGE

This French word literally means 'varnishing' and refers to the opening of an exhibition of paintings at a gallery when the artist used to put on the final coat of varnish. In training terms you conduct a vernissage when you ask participants to visit the 'gallery' of each other's work after any kind of group brainstorming session, and place question mark stickers on things they don't understand and heart stickers on things they like. A spokesperson from each group then clarifies the questions ….and only the questions!

This way everyone takes away much more from each other's work and you avoid the classic (and often un-listened to) group presentations. You can even ask them to vote for the idea they like best.

UNIVERSAL EXERCISE DESIGNS

T-SHIRT RECAP

Very simple and great fun!

- Split the group into small teams of 3-5
- Give each team a (cheap!) plain, white, XL T-shirt and a set of markers
- Ask the teams to make a representation (using keywords and images) of the main learning points you wish them to recap ON the T-shirt
- Get them to elect a *model* who will parade, fashion-show-like, in front of the other teams who may then ask questions if there are any unintelligible or otherwise dubious markings!

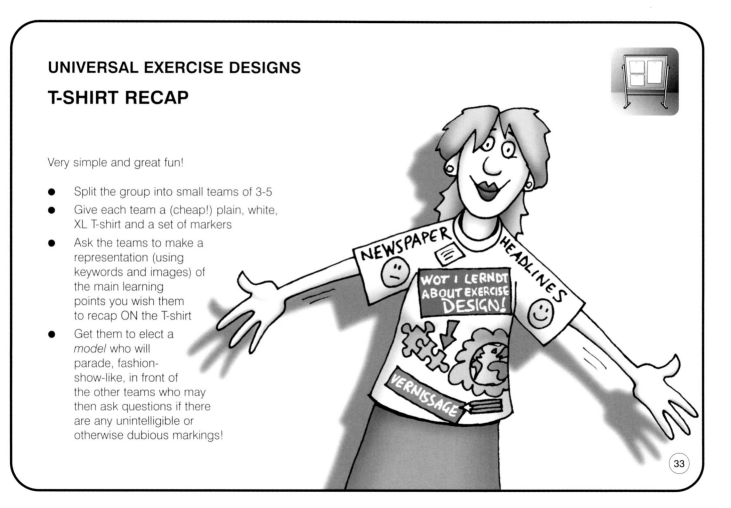

NEWSPAPER HEADLINES

Another great recap device!

- Split the group into small teams
- Give each team at least one flip chart sheet and markers
- Ask each team to create the front page of today's newspaper, reporting on what has been happening at the training course – as if the various learning points were front page news!

 As with mind mapping, you may want to ask the teams to present their final masterpieces in vernissage mode (see page 32)

SPOT-CHECKS

SPOT-CHECKS
DEFINITION

A spot-check is an instrument which can be used at any time during a training course to check on each participant's evaluation of any aspect of the process. The participant gives this evaluation by sticking a *spot* (self-adhesive dot) onto a pre-prepared grid or rating scale.

- First, draw the relevant grid on a flip chart. Next, give a self-adhesive dot to each participant. Now ask each in turn (or by group) to place their dot on the chart at the spot which represents their rating/evaluation
- For two-dimensional spot-checks this means giving opinions on two criteria by sticking the dot at the place where the ratings meet
- For three-dimensional versions (horizontal) participants use counters instead of dots and add height to show their rating of a third criterion

Look for clusters of dots in consensus zones (clouds) and for extreme individual ratings. With two- and three-dimensional spot-checks, you'll be hoping for ratings in the top right-hand quadrant. Clouds in other quadrants will be the signal to modify your approach, and isolated ratings elsewhere should prompt you to identify and speak to the person(s) concerned.

On the next six pages are two examples of each type (one-, two- and three-dimensional). The number of spot-check possibilities is limitless!

SPOT-CHECKS

ONE-DIMENSIONAL
HAPPY?

Use as an icebreaker or as a *before/after* exercise to test how participants feel at the beginning and/or at the end of any module or session.

- Draw these five faces on the flip chart, leaving space to the right for the spot-check
- Ask participants to decide which face best describes their present feelings (about the course or in general) and to come and stick their self-adhesive *spot* next to it
- To ensure a secret *ballot*, turn the flip chart around and ask participants to come up one by one

SPOT-CHECKS

ONE-DIMENSIONAL
SPEED OF COURSE?

Use to check how participants feel about the tempo of the course.

- Draw the speedometer on the flip chart
- Ask participants to decide upon their rating before coming up to stick their *spot* at the point on the speedometer pie chart which best represents their rating
- To ensure a *secret ballot*, turn the flip chart around and ask participants to come up one by one

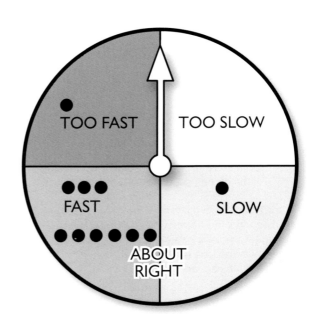

TWO-DIMENSIONAL
INTEREST/USEFULNESS

Use this two-dimensional spot-check to measure how interested the participants are in the subject matter against its usefulness to them back on the job.

- Draw the grid on a flip chart and ask participants to note down two ratings:

    1. On a scale of 1-10 (10 = high), how **interested** are you *personally* in the course subject matter?

    2. On a scale of 1-10, how **useful/applicable** is the course subject matter to your work?

- One by one, ask them to come up and place their *spot* at the point where their two ratings meet (example: a 5 rating for Interest and a 5 rating for Job Use would be placed in the middle of the *square*)

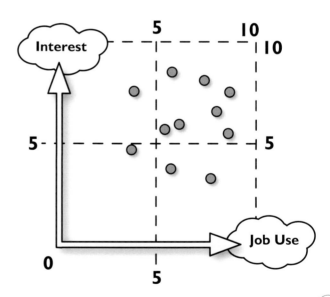

SPOT-CHECKS

TWO-DIMENSIONAL
THEORY/PRACTICE

Use to measure the participants' satisfaction with the amount of theory you are providing on the course as opposed to the opportunity to practise the new knowledge or skills.

- Draw the grid on a flip chart and ask participants to note down two ratings

  1. On a scale of 1-10 (10 = high), how satisfied are you with the amount of **theory** provided in the course?

  2. On a scale of 1-10, how satisfied are you with the amount of opportunity **to practise** the new knowledge or skills?

- One by one, ask them to come up and place their *spot* at the point where their two ratings meet

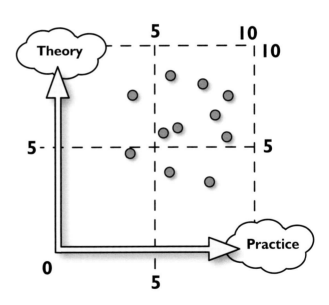

THREE-DIMENSIONAL
CONTENT/INSTRUCTOR/FACILITIES

This three-dimensional spot-check will allow participants to give you an overall rating of the course at a glance.

- Using the same principles as on pages 37 – 40, ask them to place a *counter* at the place where their ratings of the **course content** and of the **instructor** meet

- By piling up to 10 counters on top of each other they can give a *3D* rating of the conference room, and/or other **facilities**

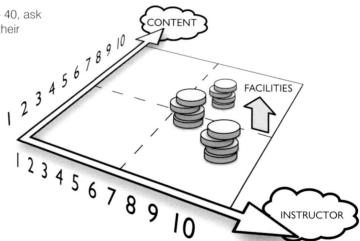

THREE-DIMENSIONAL
RESULTS/EFFORT/SATISFACTION

Use in workshop and teambuilding type courses to obtain participants' evaluation of the results they or their team achieved, the effort required and personal satisfaction gained.

- Using the same principles as on pages 37 – 40, ask them to place a counter at the place where their ratings of the **results** and the **effort** meet

- By piling up to 10 counters on top of each other they can give a *3D* **personal satisfaction** rating

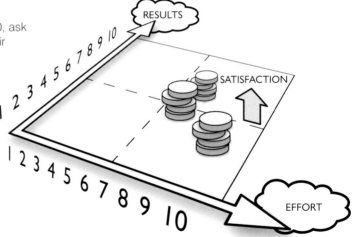

TEAMBUILDING ACTIVITIES

TEAMBUILDING ACTIVITIES

ABOUT THIS SECTION

Teambuilding is an essential part of modern management. Gone are the days when an order-giving manager could run a unit using only his/her competence and a structured staff of obedient subordinates. Today, effective management means sharing power and authority to lead a team of highly qualified people (with different skills and large egos!) to meet planned objectives. The exercises in this chapter will help accelerate the teambuilding process in the following areas:

- Team role clarification
- Interdependence of members
- Team leadership expectations

- Trust and confidence building
- Group problem-solving
- Creative thinking

For each exercise/game:

Objectives are explained

A suggested time allowance is indicated

TEAMBUILDING ACTIVITIES

ROLE CLARIFICATION
JOBSCAPING

To help the team clarify who does what.
To encourage synergy and to avoid duplication of roles/tasks.

To establish mutual expectations within the team.

Allow half a day

1. Ask each team member to write down and then present:
   - The **mission** of their job (purpose)
   - The **strategy** (how they or the organisation have decided to do it) and
   - Two to five **critical activities** currently being done

2. Encourage other team members to discuss overlaps and disagreements. For each member, the team should answer these two questions:
   - 'What should she/he *keep doing*?'
   - 'What should she/he *stop doing*?'

3. Draw up a team action plan specifying who will do/change what and by when.

Developed by Maurice Lewis of Team Training International

INTERDEPENDENCE OF MEMBERS
BUILDING A SKILLS INVENTORY

To establish what skills, abilities and personal qualities exist in a team and to encourage team members to be assertive about their contribution.

15 minutes

1. Ask team members to list those skills, abilities and personal attributes which they bring to the team.

2. Ask them to rate each item as **high** or **low** in terms of:
   - **Usefulness to team**
   - **Uniqueness in team**

3. Ask them to transfer **high/high** items to a card or Post-it (using a keyword).

4. Stick all cards/Post-its in top right hand quadrant of *spot-check* grid as illustrated, to emphasise both the opportunities for synergy which exist in the team and the advantages of interdependence.

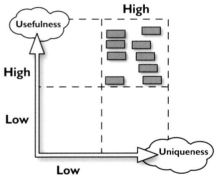

Developed by Hans Laubach/Herbert König of Team Training International

LEADERSHIP EXPECTATIONS

To help the team leader clarify what the team members expect of him/her as a leader and to obtain (if desired) a rating of present performance against those expectations.

1 hour

1. Split team members into groups of three to four and ask them to brainstorm for 30 minutes the **characteristics of a good team leader**. In other words, what are the measurable things a good team leader **is or does?**

2. Ask them to write a maximum of 15 keywords (one per characteristic) onto cards/Post-its which they should put up on the board and present to the rest of the team.

3. After presentations, help the whole team to categorise the cards, add, modify and avoid overlapping ideas.

4. During a short break, draw up a master checklist of characteristics and photocopy or print out one for each member.

5. If the team leader desires, ask each member to give him/her an *anonymous* rating from 1 (low) to 10 (high) on each item of the checklist.

BUILDING TRUST & CONFIDENCE
BILLETS DOUX

To give team members some immediate positive feedback from colleagues. To re-motivate a team which is losing its *sparkle*. To help people feel good about themselves.

15-30 minutes

1. Sit the team at a round table or in a U-shape and give each team member the same number of A6 cards (or pieces of paper) as there are members in the team.

2. Play some relaxing, non-intrusive music and ask each person to prepare one card for each of the other members. On this card, he or she should write in large, legible letters at least one strength, quality, skill or attribute which he/she particularly appreciates about that person. A keyword is sufficient but you should encourage members to expand and give specifics wherever possible.

   NB They should not give their own names, only the name of the colleague to whom the card is addressed.

3. Collect all the cards and redistribute them to the members concerned. Allow some moments for them to read their cards and then take a break.

TEAMBUILDING ACTIVITIES

PROBLEM-SOLVING
WHO DOES WHAT?

To demonstrate the need for a systematic approach to group problem-solving when all team members have the same information. *'Who does what?'* is a purely logical (left-brained) problem and might best be solved working alone!

15-20 minutes

Trainer Guide

1. First try and solve the problem yourself!

2. From the accompanying CD print off the *'Who does what?'* list of clues – one per participant.

3. Divide participants into groups of 4-7 and allow them 15-20 minutes to solve the problem.

4. Reconvene and discuss:
    ● What helped them to succeed or fail
    ● How they could have done better
    ● What they have learned about working in teams

NB The fastest and most efficient way to solve this problem is to draw-up a **complete** matrix with the people on the left and **all** the professions, sports and home towns on the top. Then tick boxes with *yes/no* (remember for each *yes* there are also four *no's!*).

PROBLEM-SOLVING
WHO DOES WHAT?

SOLUTION

| CHRISTINE |
| ANNA |
| CHARLES |
| PAUL |
| VINCENT |

PROFESSION	SPORT	HOME TOWN
CHEMIST	CYCLING	BRUSSELS
SCHOOL MISTRESS	ROCK-CLIMBING	BERLIN
CIVIL ENGINEER	WALKING	LONDON
PROFESSOR	WINDSURFING	AMSTERDAM
STUDENT	SWIMMING	PARIS

CLUE CARD

The following clues will help you to find the **profession**, the favourite **sport** and the **home town** of Christine, Anna, Charles, Paul and Vincent. You have 20 minutes to discover who does what and where.

 One of them is a school mistress

 Christine doesn't come from Paris

 Anna is from Berlin and practises rock-climbing

 Charles is a civil engineer

 Paul likes windsurfing

 Vincent does not come from London

 The Parisian says he likes swimming, the man from London is a keen walker and the cyclist is a chemist

 The student comes neither from Amsterdam nor Berlin nor Brussels

 The gentleman from Amsterdam is a professor but does not like swimming

WHO DOES WHAT?

CREATIVE THINKING
ARCHAEOLOGY

To allow a team to explore the mechanics of creative thinking by going outside the boundaries of day-to-day work and finding creative solutions to an unusual problem.

45 minutes

- Divide the team into a minimum of three groups and set them all the following problem:

  It is the year 4083 and your archaeology group has just unearthed this coin (give one to each group).

  What can you deduce about the civilization which produced this coin? Come back in 30 minutes and present your findings.

- Reconvene and ask each group to present

- If you wish to promote competitiveness or reward creativity, give each group 5 points to award to the others' presentations – in any way they see fit. Total points and award prize to the 'best'

CREATIVE THINKING
TIES

To allow a team to explore the mechanics of creative thinking by going outside the boundaries of day-to-day work and finding creative solutions to an unusual problem.

45 minutes

- Divide the team into a minimum of three groups and set them all the following problem:

  Because of a mix-up in their 5-year plan, Cuban clothing factories have produced a 2,000,000 surplus of very unfashionable men's ties made of polyester. They have been offered to your government at a very low price. Your group has been asked by the government to propose as many viable and profitable ways of using the ties as possible, before deciding whether or not to buy the consignment. You have 30 minutes.

- Reconvene and ask each group to present their best 3-4 ideas

- If you wish to promote competitiveness or reward creativity, give each group 5 points to award to the other groups' ideas – in any way they see fit. Total points and award prize to the 'best'

TEAMBUILDING ACTIVITIES
CREATIVE THINKING
ATLANTIS

To explore the mechanics of creative thinking by going outside the boundaries of day-to-day work and finding creative solutions to an unusual problem. Atlantis also allows the team to practise consensus decision-making.

45 minutes

Trainer Guide

1. Familiarise yourself with the exercise by creating your own Atlantis flag!

2. For each participant print off from the accompanying CD the Instructions Card and Flag page.

3. Distribute printed pages and sets of coloured pencils to each participant. Allow 10 minutes for Phase 1.

4. Break team into a minimum of three groups and allow 30 minutes for Phase 2.

5. Reconvene and ask spokesperson from each group to present their flag.

6. Give each group 5 points to award to the other groups' flags in any way they see fit. Total points and award prize.

Things to look for

● What behaviours helped or hindered the groups in reaching consensus?
● What style was used by the leader to guide the groups?
● Which team members contributed most/least and why?
● How did the groups deal with conflicting opinions?

Be sure to get each group's analysis of all the above points and ask spokespeople what they have learned about creative thinking in groups.

INSTRUCTIONS CARD

The geological miracle of the reappearance of the lost continent of Atlantis is still astounding and exciting scientists, politicians and, of course, the general public. Now that the lava has cooled and plants are beginning to take root, the United Nations has put an end to quarrels over the possible sovereignty of the 6th continent by proposing that an intercontinental task force be sent to 'colonize' the new land. As you know, Atlantis emerged from the mid-Atlantic ridge on the Tropic of Cancer (about half-way between Morocco and Florida) and is roughly the size of Iceland.

The plan is for each continent to select 100 young men and women volunteers to settle on Atlantis and build a civilization. These 500 pioneers will be the founding fathers and mothers of a new planetary race and culture – the representatives of global peace and harmony. As one of the first steps, the United Nations has asked your group to design a flag for Atlantis!

Phase ❶   *Working alone, you have 10 minutes to rough out one or several ideas for the flag using the coloured pencils provided by the trainer. You may use any criteria you wish in your choice of symbols/colours.*

Phase ❷   *When the trainer invites you to join your group, you will have 30 minutes to produce and present on a flip chart a collective, final design for the Atlantis flag – one which every member accepts as being representative of the group's thinking. This is an exercise in creative problem-solving and consensus-seeking.*

Guidelines   ● The most important decision for the group will be: *How are we going to make our decision?!*
● Listen to the others
● Work for the interest of the group (and Atlantis) but don't let your ideas and feelings be sacrificed too easily.

Although there will be no winners and losers, allow yourself 1 point for every 'idea' included in the final flag which you can trace to your original design.

ATLANTIS

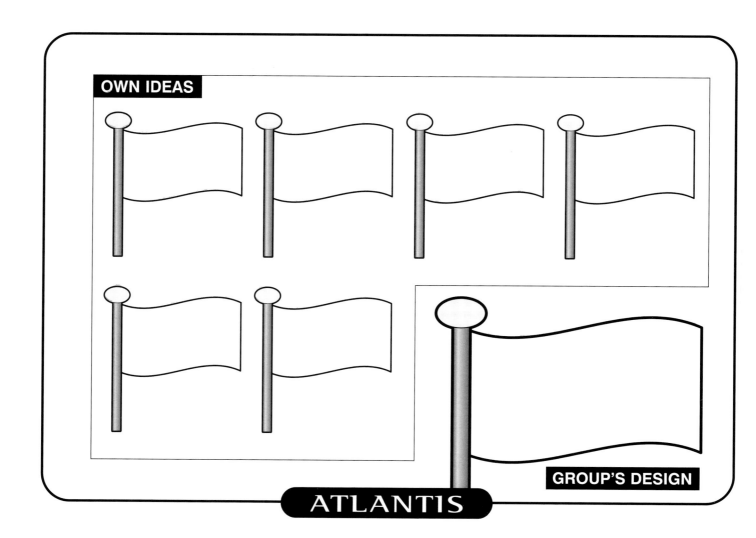

WESTREK
<u>PLANNING</u>

WESTREK

TRAINER'S GUIDE

To teach the five essential steps in the planning of any project. To demonstrate the need for co-operation, sharing and synergy in a team – especially during the planning of a project.

90 minutes

1. Familiarise yourself with the team instructions and with the Map and the 19 Clue Cards. Go through the Solution (page 59) using the Map and the Clue Cards as a guide. Make up appropriate number of card sets (page 60).

2. Divide the participants into teams of 5-7 members and explain the objectives of the Westrek exercise.

3. Distribute a Team Instructions Card and a Map to each member of each team.

4. While they are reading the instructions, shuffle and deal at random one set of Clue Cards to each team.

5. Locate each team in a separate room, allow approximately 30 minutes to answer the six questions, then reconvene.

6. Ask one team for their solution and check agreement from others.

7. Go through review questions on page 82 with each team.

WESTREK

SOLUTION

- **Where are we coming from?**
  25 km south of Finger Rock
  (Cards G, I and J)

- **Where are we now?**
  Finger Rock *(Card G)*

- **Where are we heading?**
  Towards Turquoise Trading Post
  (Card H)

- **Where do we want to be?**
  Sparroweye *(Cards D, E and F)*

- **By when?**
  July 12th *(Cards A and C)*

- **How will we get there?**
  Best route is: Western Trail, Eagle Pass *(Card B)*, build a raft *(Card P)*, Wood River *(Card M)*,
  San José River *(Cards L and O)*. You can't cross it but why not float down!

  But, you could play safe and leave raft near Buzzard and walk to Sparroweye (one day longer).

  Not via Kestrel Lake *(Card N)* or Satan's Cauldron *(Card Q)*.

  Shortest time is six days: two days to *first trees*, one day to build raft, three days to Sparroweye *(Card K)*.

PREPARATION

1. From the accompanying CD print off a Team Instructions Card and Map for each participant.

2. Now print off a set of Clue Cards for each team of 5-7 members, changing the colour of the paper for each set of 19 cards.

TEAM INSTRUCTIONS CARD

You and your group are following a management training course in the USA. Part of the training course consists of a *Westrek Survival Exercise* in the Wild West!

The group has been taken in a closed helicopter on a night flight and has been dropped at an unknown location. Each of you has a back-pack with a sleeping bag, enough food and survival rations for 10 days, water for two days, a watch, a compass, an axe and 10 metres of rope.

The pilot of the helicopter gave each team member an envelope before taking off in the sudden light of dawn at 06.00 am. He explained that you should all start walking towards a natural landmark on the horizon and that, at noon precisely, you should stop and open your envelopes.

It is now noon, you have reached the landmark and you have all just opened your envelopes. As you can see, they contain a number of Clue Cards – some explicit, some enigmatic – and a Map of the area in which you have been dropped.

1 *Instructions*

The group must stay at the present location for 30 minutes to discuss the information on each member's Clue Cards and to answer the following questions precisely:

- *Where are we coming from?* - *(Mark helicopter landing spot on Map)*
- *Where are we now?* - *(Mark present location on Map)*
- *Where are we heading if we keep going as now?* - *(Mark present direction and likely destination on Map)*
- *Where do we want to be?* - *(Circle the planned destination/objective)*
- *By when do we want to be there?* - *(What is the deadline?)*
- *How will we get there in the shortest possible time?* - *(Trace route on Map and calculate duration of journey)*

2 You **must** share the information on your Clue Cards with the other team members but please don't show the cards themselves or write on them.

Thanks and good luck!

Today there will be fireworks and celebrations throughout the United States

Hannibal
did it with elephants!

c

The pilot says he'll wait for you until July 12th at your destination

The phantom goal is a derelict town

WESTREK

You must reach
the place the French call
'L'oeil du Moineau'

Twenty and twice six plus two leads to goal (from the opposite direction)

You are now at the place the Navaho call 'The Pointing Stone'

If you keep heading in the same direction at the same speed as this morning, you can buy a blue-green necklace for your loved one at 16.15 hours

WESTREK

If you have reached the landmark, you have covered 25 kilometres from the place where the helicopter left you

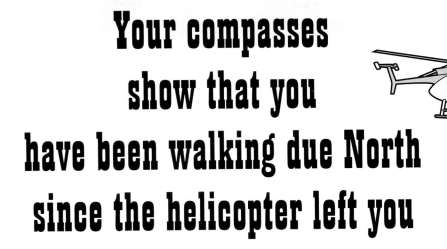

Your compasses show that you have been walking due North since the helicopter left you

The Indians say:
'From first trees to Tepees, the sunrises are three'

It is impossible to <u>cross</u> the San José River

Little running water from great bird's nest soothes and speeds the weary Indian's return

Little running water from still water is the enemy of the returning traveller

Great running water
is faster than a horse and cannot
be crossed

Finn and Sawyer did it — why can't you?

The evil one's boiling pot is the graveyard of many a returning brave

WESTREK

R

- **Answer each question on the Instructions Card, one at a time**

- **Share all information**

- **The letters on the top of the cards have no significance**

WESTREK

Of course,
it's easier to walk on roads!

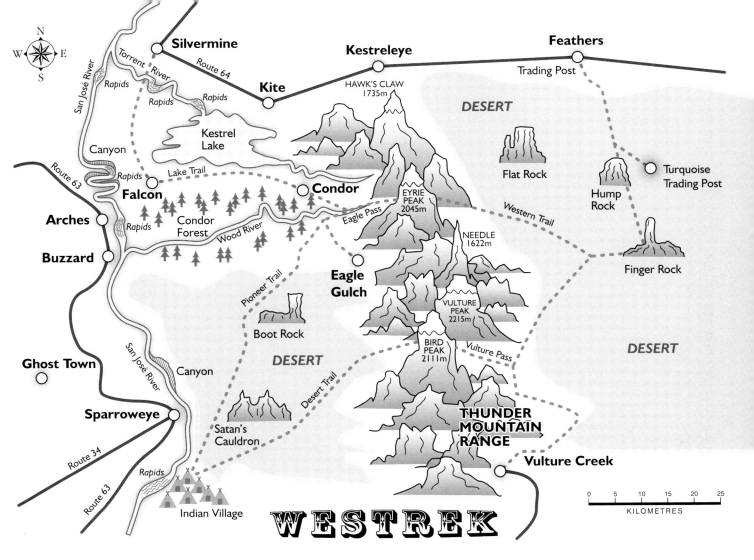

WESTREK

TRAINER'S REVIEW GUIDE

During the exercise, make sure you spend time with each group to observe the way in which they go about tackling the problem. This is not, in principle, a group dynamics or leadership exercise. It is designed to help groups become conscious of the steps to successful planning. Things to look and listen for:

● Do they answer each of the six questions in order? *(Card R)*

● To what extent do they go straight to the objective/destination before knowing where they are coming from/heading or where they are now? (Typical planning session error)

● Do they answer the question, 'Where are we heading – if we keep going as now?' correctly? Most groups forget that, in real life, present direction can impact greatly on the feasibility of an objective or deadline

● To what extent do they use **all** the information before taking a decision?

During the review session ask each group to comment on the WAY in which they solved the problem (process) and give your comments on any of the above.

FOREST FIRE

CONSENSUS–SEEKING

FOREST FIRE

TRAINER'S GUIDE

To study the impact of individual attitudes and values or prejudices on team decision-making, and to practise consensus-seeking behaviours and methods.

90 minutes

1. Familiarise yourself with the Team Instructions Card and the résumés of the 10 volunteers. Make your own *personal rescue sequence* to get the feel of the exercise. Create an appropriate number of handouts (see page 85).

2. Distribute a set of handouts to each participant and ask them to make their own *personal rescue sequence* (10 minutes). Invite any participant who finds the exercise unethical or distasteful to withdraw and/or become an observer.

3. Divide the participants into small groups of 5-7 and ask them to appoint a leader. Allow 50 minutes for the groups to arrive at a *group rescue sequence* as per the instructions.

4. Reconvene in a plenary session to review the exercise (see *Trainer's Review Guide* on page 98).

FOREST FIRE
PREPARATION

1. For each participant, print off from the accompanying CD a Team Instructions Card, a Rescue Sequence sheet and a set of the 10 résumé cards.

TEAM INSTRUCTIONS CARD

Your group is a helicopter rescue team, responsible for organising air/land rescues over a specified geographical area. A forest fire of unprecedented violence has broken out in an uninhabited region of thickly wooded foothills in the south west of your area. The only buildings in this vast area are five isolated wooden chalets which were built during the last war as look-out posts. They are now used exclusively as base camps for volunteers from all over the world who have been hired by the International Parks Commission to spend some of their free time surveying and evaluating the terrain for use as a World Recreation Centre.

Each chalet has a radio link with your rescue centre. Your team has already assigned four of the tiny rescue helicopters to evacuate chalet numbers 1-4 and they cannot be re-diverted.

The team's present task is to evacuate the people in chalet no. 5

1 No other rescue means are at your disposal. You have contacted the group spokesperson in the chalet and have been informed that the fire is raging within a few kilometres and has completely surrounded the chalet.

2 The group has been told that your helicopter can only rescue one person at a time. Each flight to safe, higher ground and back to the chalet will take at least 10 minutes, so it is likely that the fire will reach and destroy the chalet before all 10 volunteers have been rescued. You estimate that five or six rescues may be feasible but the pilot says he may only be able to get three or four people out before the fire reaches the chalet. The group in the chalet are unwilling to take the decision as to the sequence in which they should be rescued.

3 Your team leader has told you that you have a total of 60 minutes to take this unpleasant decision while the helicopter and the pilot are being prepared, and has asked each of you to take 10 minutes to establish a *personal rescue sequence* by ranking names in order from 1 (first) to 10 (last) before discussing the problem as a group and reaching a consensus on the ranking. Please note your decision by writing the names in the *Personal* column of the *Rescue Sequence* sheet. Leave the *Group* column blank until the group has come to a consensus. The only information available on each volunteer is on his/her résumé card which is included here and which comes from the IPC confidential personnel files. You may use any criteria you wish in making your decision.

FOREST FIRE

RESCUE SEQUENCE

Personal	Group
1	
2	
3	
4	
5	
6	
7	
8	
9	
10	

FOREST FIRE

Name: **PATRICK**

Profile: Patrick is 44 years old and has been divorced for two years. Since the divorce, Patrick has unfortunately taken to drinking heavily and has just been released from a two-month prison sentence for drink-driving (he owns a very fast Ferrari). Patrick was born in Ireland but now lives in Mayfair. He is presently a professor at one of London's leading colleges of dental surgery and has recently achieved a worldwide reputation by pioneering a revolutionary new method for preventing dental decay. He has decided to join the World Health Organisation in Geneva and dedicate his further research to the adaptation of this method for use by dentists in developing countries. Much of his research is still in his work notebooks.

Name: **WOLFGANG**

Profile: Wolfgang is an unmarried 28 year old German who works as a physical training instructor at a fitness centre in Munich. His hobby is weight-lifting and he has twice won the title of Bayerische Landesmeister (Bavarian Area Champion) in his category.

He left school at 16 to join the merchant navy and is now known to hold fairly extreme right-wing political views.

Name: **MARIA**

Profile: Maria is a 17 year old Spanish girl from a very wealthy industrial family in Barcelona. She is presently at a finishing school in Lausanne. Her parents would like her to marry into an old Spanish aristocratic family with whom she has recently been on a yachting vacation to the Greek islands, and who have a castle near her parents' estate.

So far, Maria has expressed no alternative life goals and it is possible that the marriage be arranged immediately after her return from this vacation.

Name: **MAMADOU**

Profile: Mamadou is a married man of 39 years who was born in Senegal (West Africa). He is a devout Muslim and a founder member of the Société pour la préservation de la culture Sénégalaise in Dakar where he lives.

He is a novelist and poet by profession and has nine children whose ages range from 4 to 19. His hobbies include playing in a local folk music group.

Name: **INGRID**

Profile: Ingrid is a 25 year old Swedish girl who has just brilliantly completed her PhD in Human Biology. She has received an unpublicised offer and grant from the Swedish government to conduct research into cloning and genetics control.

She is exceptionally attractive with a good figure and, being from a poor family, was able to help pay for her costly studies by occasionally posing for nude magazines.

Name: **WILLI**

Profile: Willi is a 52 year old Belgian school teacher. He is single and is head geography teacher at a private boys' boarding school in Antwerp. He created the Boy Scout Troop at the school and has dedicated all his spare time to organising field trips, visits to museums and summer camps for groups of up to 50 young scouts.

Unfortunately, he was recently involved in a successfully hushed-up scandal about complaints from several parents that he had had minor sexual experiences with their 8-10 year olds. It is not clear whether there is any truth in these allegations.

FOREST FIRE

Name: **WILBUR**

Profile: Wilbur is a 57 year old American who has lived in Pittsburgh all his life. He is a self-made man and is Vice-President, Manufacturing for a machine-tool company employing 750 people. He is a member of the Round Table and his wife, Harriet, is one of the Daughters of the American Revolution.

Wilbur and Harriet have two grown-up sons who have married and moved to California. Wilbur is personally responsible for obtaining signatures on an important contract with a French customer which will result, if signed, in the creation of a further 400 jobs back at the plant. He is staunchly anti-British and is half-way through writing a book on the American War of Independence.

Name: **RAJI**

Profile: Raji is a 38 year old married Pakistani with seven children (aged 4-15) who has been living in England for 10 years. Although he is a qualified accounting clerk, he has been living on unemployment benefits and social security for the last five years.

He recently converted to Christianity and has secured a job with the Civil Service to start in two months. He decided to volunteer for this IPC assignment to clear his mind before making a fresh start in life.

FOREST FIRE

Name: **MARIE-FRANCE**

Profile: Marie-France is a 33 year old French housewife. She has three children aged 16 months, 3 and 5 years. She lives in a pleasant middle-class suburb of Paris and her hobbies are cooking and going to pop music concerts.

She is known to be having an affair with another of the volunteers (Wolfgang).

FOREST FIRE

Name: **AHMED**

Profile: Ahmed is of Algerian nationality and is married with six children. He is 35 years old and known to be a member of the outlawed FIS (the Algerian Islamic Fundamentalist Front).

He holds very strong views on women's roles in society and has had some serious clashes with Ingrid and Marie-France, not to mention Wolfgang. It is not clear why he volunteered for the IPC project.

FOREST FIRE

FOREST FIRE

TRAINER'S REVIEW GUIDE

The Forest Fire exercise deals with very sensitive issues – personal values and prejudices – and team members are asked to make what they may consider impossible decisions. However, if they agree to *play the game* (and if the instructor is a qualified facilitator) they can learn a great deal about consensus-seeking, group dynamics and teambuilding.

The only *safe* way to reach group consensus is to agree on selection criteria. These may include responsibility for dependants, age (lowest first), contribution to society (difficult!), etc. The easiest and most dispassionate method is to make a matrix with criteria on the left and the volunteers along the top and to score each volunteer against each criterion, then add up the points.

Things to look for

- What actions/behaviours helped or hindered the groups in reaching consensus?
- What style was used by the official (and unofficial) leaders to guide the groups?
- Which team members contributed most/least and why?
- To what extent were personal feelings expressed/suppressed?
- How did the groups deal with conflicting opinions?

Be sure to get each group's analysis of all of the above points and ask spokespeople what they have learned about working in a team.

TESTS & QUIZZES

TESTS & QUIZZES
QUESTIONNAIRES

Use *home-made* questionnaires as a quick way to:

- Identify participants' knowledge level at the **start** of a course
- Check understanding of learning points **during** a course
- Test knowledge acquisition at the **end** of a course

For ease of administration and analysis, make sure that your design uses:

- Closed questions (one possible answer only) OR
- Forced choice questions (one choice from 3-6 possibilities)

To measure attitudes or opinions, use clear questions with clearly defined attitude choices (if you ask open questions it will be difficult to compare and analyse responses). Use either forced choice boxes to check (ie: excellent, good, poor, terrible) or provide a sliding scale and ask participants to place a cross on the line. Example:

Strongly agree   Agree   Disagree   Strongly disagree

NB Providing only four choices stops people *sitting on the fence* by rating in the middle.

Remember, the information you get is only as good as the question you ask.

RECAP TEST
THE KEY-WORD CROSSWORD PUZZLE

A fun way to test participants' retention of knowledge. Decide on a key-word which has dominated the learning experience and write it in horizontal crossword squares. Now find other words which summarise points to be remembered from the course and fit them <u>vertically</u> into the key-word. Next, create clues for each of the words and draw up the blank puzzle.

Distribute copies to be completed individually or in groups. Clues for the example opposite could be:

- To find out whose pocketbook this is, fill in the blanks with these clues:
    1. Chapter 3 helps build this
    2. An exercise in rafting!
    3. Name of flag activity in this book
    4. Another way of testing retention
    5. What the answer to number 2 teaches
    6. Head person in a team
    7. What to do after each module
    8. A kind of check

THE RECAP QUIZ GAME

I've never met a participant who didn't enjoy a good quiz game! From managing directors to truck drivers, people love to pit their wits against each other.

Here's a simple Quiz Game design for any course:

1. Prepare 10-20 questions on A6 cards (or pieces of paper), each with the same number of components (1-5). *Examples: Name 3 major competitors. Give 3 features of this new product. Name 3 likely objections.*

2. Divide participants into teams of 2-5. Name teams.

3. Start with team on left. Read first question. Allow 15 seconds to confer. Score answer on pre-prepared flip chart (nice TV show artwork please!). If any component is wrong, allow next team (or first team to raise hand) to try for bonus point(s).

4. Read second question to second team and so on.

5. Award prize to winning team.

THE RECAP QUIZ GAME
VARIATIONS

Here are some variations of The Recap Quiz Game (previous page) that you can try:

- Prepare questions in difficulty levels and allow each team to choose a level (more/less points)

- Create 4-5 different rounds each with different sorts of questions

- If you only have two teams and want a really noisy and fast-moving quiz, place two flip charts at front of class and get each team to elect a scribe. Angle flips so scribes can't see each other's flip but audience can see both. Place a waste-paper bin between flips. Read questions to both groups. The first scribe to write the correct answer on flip and place/throw pen into the bin gets the point(s). Scribes may confer (silently) with their team. No other rules are needed!

TESTS & QUIZZES

SUPERSTAR TEST & ACTION PLAN

- To be used at the beginning or end of skills and behavioural courses to establish criteria against which to plan for change.

1. Divide the participants into groups of 3-7.

2. Ask each group to identify the TOP 10 characteristics/skills of the Superstar (of whatever discipline/role – eg: trainer, presenter, coach, etc) and ask the group to transfer the information to Post-its and to stick these on the whiteboard/flip.

3. Discuss and eliminate overlaps. Agree on final list of 15-20 characteristics/skills.

4. During the coffee break, print off from the accompanying CD the Superstar Grid and enter the characteristics/skills in the appropriate column (paraphrasing first, if necessary).

5. Make a photocopy of the completed grid for each participant and distribute.

6. Ask each participant to rate him/herself against each of the characteristics/skills by ticking the appropriate box on the grid's rating scale, where 1 is the lowest rating and 10 is the highest.

7. Finally, join up the ticks to obtain a Superstar profile and then draw up an **action plan** on how to improve upon the lowest 3-5 rated characteristics/skills.

14.
15. Starts with icebreaker
16. Uses colour on all slides
17. Uses these exercises!
18. Reflects/deflects
19. Recaps all modules
20. Uses spot-checks

Action plan: Use at least one spot-check per programme.

SUPERSTAR GRID

Superstar characteristics/skills

Rating Scale

	1	2	3	4	5	6	7	8	9	10
1.	☐	☐	☐	☐	☐	☐	☐	☐	☐	☐
2.	☐	☐	☐	☐	☐	☐	☐	☐	☐	☐
3.	☐	☐	☐	☐	☐	☐	☐	☐	☐	☐
4.	☐	☐	☐	☐	☐	☐	☐	☐	☐	☐
5.	☐	☐	☐	☐	☐	☐	☐	☐	☐	☐
6.	☐	☐	☐	☐	☐	☐	☐	☐	☐	☐
7.	☐	☐	☐	☐	☐	☐	☐	☐	☐	☐
8.	☐	☐	☐	☐	☐	☐	☐	☐	☐	☐
9.	☐	☐	☐	☐	☐	☐	☐	☐	☐	☐
10.	☐	☐	☐	☐	☐	☐	☐	☐	☐	☐
11.	☐	☐	☐	☐	☐	☐	☐	☐	☐	☐
12.	☐	☐	☐	☐	☐	☐	☐	☐	☐	☐
13.	☐	☐	☐	☐	☐	☐	☐	☐	☐	☐
14.	☐	☐	☐	☐	☐	☐	☐	☐	☐	☐
15.	☐	☐	☐	☐	☐	☐	☐	☐	☐	☐
16.	☐	☐	☐	☐	☐	☐	☐	☐	☐	☐
17.	☐	☐	☐	☐	☐	☐	☐	☐	☐	☐
18.	☐	☐	☐	☐	☐	☐	☐	☐	☐	☐
19.	☐	☐	☐	☐	☐	☐	☐	☐	☐	☐
20.	☐	☐	☐	☐	☐	☐	☐	☐	☐	☐

Action plan:

THE 7 WONDERS MEMORY TEST

Ever wondered how to remember the 7 Wonders of the World!? All you have to do is to think of a football team called the **L Champs**.

Here's how to use the memory test as an icebreaker, an energizer or to prove a point:

- Ask participants how many of the 7 Wonders they can think of (few!). Write on flip
- Show the L Champs T-shirt on a transparency or on the flip and explain how the acronym works
- Test their memory again!
- To prove the effectiveness of memory devices like this, test again on day 2!

L ighthouse at Alexandria
C olossus of Rhodes
H anging Gardens of Babylon
A rtemis' Temple at Ephesus
M ausoleum at Halicarnassus
P yramids
S tatue of Zeus at Olympia

ABOUT THE AUTHOR

John Townsend, BA MA MCIPD

John has built a reputation internationally as a leading trainer of trainers. He is the founder of the highly-regarded Master Trainer Institute, a *total learning* facility located just outside Geneva which draws trainers and facilitators from around the world. He set up the Institute after 30 years' experience in international consulting and human resource management positions in the UK, France, the United States and Switzerland.

From 1978–1984 he was European Director of Executive Development with GTE in Geneva with training responsibility for over 800 managers in some 15 countries. John has published a number of management and professional guides and regularly contributes articles to leading management and training journals.

In addition to training trainers, he is also a regular speaker at conferences and leadership seminars throughout Europe.

Contact

John Townsend, The Master Trainer Institute,
L'Avant Centre, 13 chemin du Levant, Ferney-Voltaire, France
Tel: (33) 450 42 84 16   Fax: (33) 450 40 57 37
www.mt-institute.com

THE MANAGEMENT POCKETBOOK SERIES

Pocketbooks

Appraisals	Employment Law	Marketing	Succeeding at Interviews
Assertiveness	Empowerment	Meetings	Teamworking
Balance Sheet	Energy and Well-being	Mentoring	Telephone Skills
Business Planning	Facilitator's	Motivation	Telesales
Business Writing	Handling Complaints	Negotiator's	Thinker's
Call Centre Customer Care	Icebreakers	Networking	Time Management
Career Transition	Impact & Presence	NLP	Trainer Standards
Challengers	Improving Efficiency	Openers & Closers	Trainer's
Coaching	Improving Profitability	People Manager's	Training Evaluation
Communicator's	Induction	Performance Management	Training Needs Analysis
Competencies	Influencing	Personal Success	Vocal Skills
Controlling Absenteeism	International Trade	Positive Mental Attitude	
Creative Manager's	Interviewer's	Presentations	
C.R.M.	I.T. Trainer's	Problem Behaviour	**Pocketsquares**
Cross-cultural Business	Key Account Manager's	Problem Solving	Great Training Robbery
Cultural Gaffes	Leadership	Project Management	Hook Your Audience
Customer Service	Learner's	Quality	
Decision-making	Manager's	Resolving Conflict	**Pocketfiles**
Developing People	Managing Budgets	Sales Excellence	
Discipline	Managing Cashflow	Salesperson's	Trainer's Blue Pocketfile of Ready-to-use Activities
Diversity	Managing Change	Self-managed Development	
E-commerce	Managing Upwards	Starting In Management	Trainer's Green Pocketfile of Ready-to-use Activities
Emotional Intelligence	Managing Your Appraisal	Stress	
			Trainer's Red Pocketfile of Ready-to-use Activities

ORDER FORM

Your details

Name _____

Position _____

Company _____

Address _____

_____

_____

Telephone _____

Facsimile _____

E-mail _____

VAT No. (EC companies) _____

Your Order Ref _____

Please send me:

		No. copies
The	Trainer's Blue Pocketfile	☐
The	_____	☐
The	_____	☐
The	_____	☐

Order by Post
MANAGEMENT POCKETBOOKS LTD
LAUREL HOUSE, STATION APPROACH, ALRESFORD,
HAMPSHIRE SO24 9JH UK

Order by Phone, Fax or Internet
Telephone: +44 (0)1962 735573
Facsimile: +44 (0)1962 733637
E-mail: sales@pocketbook.co.uk
Web: www.pocketbook.co.uk

Customers in USA should contact:
Stylus Publishing, LLC, 22883 Quicksilver Drive,
Sterling, VA 20166-2012
Telephone: 703 661 1581 or 800 232 0223
Facsimile: 703 661 1501 E-mail: styluspub@aol.com

MANAGEMENT POCKETBOOKS